SETTING THE FIRES

OTHER TITLES FROM AIRLIE PRESS

THE EDDY FENCE *Donna Henderson*

LAST APPLES OF LATE EMPIRES *Jessica Lamb*

GARDEN OF BEASTS *Anita Sullivan*

OUT OF REFUSAL *Carter McKenzie*

ENTERING *Cecelia Hagen*

THE NEXT THING ALWAYS BELONGS *Chris Anderson*

CONGRESS OF STRANGE PEOPLE *Stephanie Lenox*

IRON STRING *Annie Lighthart*

STILL LIFE WITH JUDAS & LIGHTNING *Dawn Diez Willis*

SKEIN OF LIGHT *Karen McPherson*

PICTURE X *Tim Shaner*

PARTLY FALLEN *Deborah Akers*

SETTING THE FIRES

DARLENE PAGÁN

You are an amazing storyteller.
Keep at it. Keep us
laughing and crying
Darlene Pagán

Airlie Press
PORTLAND OREGON
2015

Airlie Press is supported by book sales, by contributions to the press from its supporters, and by the work donated by all the poet-editors of the press.

Major funding has been provided by, or on behalf of:

Julia Ryan Wills
Christine Stephenson
Cindi Kyte (in memory of Byron and Laverne Akers)
Anonymous (in memory of George Hitchcock)

P.O. BOX 82653
PORTLAND OR 97282
WWW.AIRLIEPRESS.ORG

EMAIL: EDITORS@AIRLIEPRESS.ORG

Cover Art: Laara WilliamSen, The Elements-Fire #5

Cover and Book Design: Beth Ford, Glib Communications & Design

FIRST EDITION

ISBN: 978-0-9895799-2-6

Library of Congress Control Number: 2015940337

Printed in the United States of America

For my mother, Linda Mae Sander

One must live like fire. Burn the wretchedness of days.
give warmth and light. –*Give*.

–Jean-Paul Michel

The wind shows us how close to the edge we are.

–Joan Didion

FUEL

3 How It All Started
4 Razbliuto
6 Halloween, Baptist Church, Canton, NC
7 Theft
8 Savyiore
10 Wife Still a Suspect in Blaze that Claims Husband
11 Fuel
12 The Wolf and the Kid
14 St. Anthony's Bread
15 Shooting Range
16 Setting the Fire
17 Things I've Taken a Match To
18 Akathorasbagharvakomala, A Very Soft Fabric
19 Starving the Panic

HEAT

22 St. Mary's Catholic School for Girls
23 The Driver's Test
24 The Farrier
25 On the Anniversary of Her Husband's Death, Great Aunt Irene Calls
26 Blackout
28 Hansel Alone
29 The Reel
30 Anatomy of a Girl

32 Woman Claims Hearing Loss Gives the Gift of Sight
33 The Quarry
34 Heat
35 Warding Off the Proposal
36 Once Upon a Time

BREATH

40 After the Fire
42 In College, I Job Shadow My Mother, a Hospice Nurse
44 The Uses of Grief
46 The Edge of Spring
47 The Difficult Habit of Staying Alive
48 Breath
49 Motion Study
50 This Boy, Here
52 Through the Fire
53 The Lamp
54 The Last to Go
56 The Day An Officer Shows Up Who Looks Exactly Like the Actor Gary Oldman
57 Unwanted Pepper
58 The Red Eye
59 Dark Matter
60 A Sage Advises How to Firewalk

FUEL

HOW IT ALL STARTED

By the end of the trip, she had never been
more sorry, a word he discarded like something
she'd made at summer camp—a cross between

an ashtray and a turtle. Sorry she forgot
the lantern, the towels, the hot dog buns,
the matches. Hadn't they found

a lighter? Sorry she could not fry an egg
over an open flame and not leave it all sticking
to the pan. Sorry she launched him into the river

trying to help him steady the canoe. Sorry he left it
to her to put out the fire their last morning—the one
thing, he had said, she ought to be able to get

right. Sorries in hand, she kicked dirt
on the flames, burying them deep,
then watched as the heart expanded

and pulsed back to life. Again and again,
she buried the stubborn coals, watched them
gasp for air and reignite. He slammed a car door

as an ember opened its smoking eye and trained it
on her like a dare. The ember woke another
and another as she turned to walk away.

RAZBLIUTO

I recite in the dark
Ya'aburnee, Arabic for you bury me
Fernweh, German for a longing to be away
Hyggelig, Danish for a night with cold beer
and friends before a warm fire
or *L'appel du vide*, French for the urge to jump
from high places. The words lulled me until
I stopped on *Razbliuto*, Russian for the feelings
you have for someone you once loved
but now do not. After settling the baby
who woke wet with a fever, I return

to the list of words designed to inspire
the poet who is still asleep in me
as dawn approaches. I write *Razbliuto* down
in looping, exaggerated cursive, then watch
out the window as a blue jay thieves a branch
from another nest. A black hole, the word
collapses lovers and friends
into smaller and smaller elements—

a rock from a hike, a cinnamon scent,
a letter written by a hand I once drew
stars into, then wept into even
as I forgot the texture of those fingers
on my tongue. I look the word up
only to find it doesn't exist, just
the root word, *razliubit*, to stop
loving, recorded in a long list
of urban legends like the German
Scheissenbedauern, the disappointment felt
when something turns out not nearly
as badly as one expected.

And what did I expect? The girl
who convinced her sister gnomes would visit
if she left offerings of money and chocolate
on a stump— the girl, now a mother,
who lets the baby cry a little longer
so she can corner a few bulky words, drag them
up by the ankles, and shake their pockets clean.

HALLOWEEN, BAPTIST CHURCH, CANTON, NC

The congregation cheers as each book
lands in the blaze. Hardbacks
curl like tongues, ash
confetti flying up
from the corners.
New members take turns
casting literature wrought
by Satan's hands
onto the pile:
fantasy, erotica, versions
of the bible other than
the King James.
Some books open like hands
out of which characters leap:
a Roman soldier on horseback,
Huck Finn whipping
flames with a willow branch.
A log snaps
and Emma Bovary
flutters skyward with a sigh
in a tight yellow gown.
Color prints liberate
a green-robed wizard
who dances across the center pile
until it collapses in a shower
of sparks. Some break
into song, others
speak in tongues—
voices lifting beyond
the reach of prayer
and the longing to be burned.

THEFT

The first was third grade, St. Mary's,
at the end of a week-long fundraiser: *Boys*
Battle Girls to Give to Africa. In my damp palm,

the worn ten dollar bill I'd slipped from
my mother's purse smelled like a saddle blanket.
I stood after the students dropped their change

into the enormous glass jars under a banner
with a picture of the Continent like
a hollowed thumbprint. It wasn't

that I cared about Africa. We'd eaten rice
and beans for the third time that week
and my Sunday dress became my Tuesday

and Thursday dress and the bags of fruit
the church left on our doorstep after Dad
was laid off turned to mush from an early frost.

Fist clenched, I kept my head down, tried
to look holy, even as I stepped over the feet
poking out from under desks to trip me.

The only other kid to donate paper,
Mary Rutherford glowered, mouth pinned
like the pink hem on her white dress. Above

the jar marked *Girls*, I opened my hand,
held up the money, and let it go. Hoots
and applause boomed, desktops

slammed. Later, while Sister Barbara spoke
to my mother, I muttered penance on my knees
to a ruined Christ. But when I closed my eyes,

I saw that bill fall from my hand over and over
as the cheering rose, adding up those shiny
coins and all the math I'd ever need.

SAVYIORE

According to the postmark, the Messiah
has been in Tampa all these years, promising
to reveal His personal message of salvation
if only I'd send money. The paper looks
more like a party invitation, the block
letters shimmering in neon blue and yellow
above an illegible signature in green ink.

The letter arrives with another from
an uncle in prison and covered in brown
splotches with the faint scent of vinegar.
Unlike the Messiah, my uncle
cannot spell, and he is not happy with just
any amount I can spare. He wants $57.99
to buy gym shoes after his were stolen.

He needs a sponsor too when he gets out
in a month and stamps so he can write
to any other relative whose address I would
kindly forward. He tells me, *I don't diserve*
this ~~crap~~ shit. I'm not like these ~~poeple~~ guys.
And, *You don't have to write back, just let me*
know you got this. I haven't seen my uncle

in ten years since he left with my babysitting
money to get gas after promising to teach me
how to drive a snowmobile. I'd turned
eighteen, and was born again that Sunday
for a second time. These letters
have chased me for years. At least
the Messiah includes an envelope I can reuse
with a stamp of the Virgin with open arms

looking down serenely at the address, above
which the text warns: *Now is the time to be saved!!*
My uncle swears he can save himself
if someone somewhere would just give him
the chance. He promises to look at the knock
in my engine too, when he's back in town.

WIFE STILL A SUSPECT IN BLAZE THAT CLAIMS HUSBAND

The air crackled with a lightning storm.
The chickens refused to lay

and no matter how long she kneaded
the dough, all day, the loaves cooked up

dense and hard as baseball bats.
At least no child again this month.

When she put the match to the sheet, she
never imagined it would curl him

in its hot tongue, never believed he would not
wake in those flames, throw back the covers,

and wash his feet like she'd begged him
before bed every night for years.

Now, bits of sheet, newly caught on fire
rise like cardinals. Black petals fall. A door

opens, the wind roars, timbers spit and splinter
until she finds herself outside in the grass

watching winds lash the flames.
When they pull the body, too late,

from the house, she means it when
she tells them she hardly knew the man.

FUEL

We must embrace pain and burn it as fuel.
—Kenji Miyazawa

Here is the ache strung
on the back like an infant
I've swaddled in wool
all winter and have
yet to learn to love.

Here is the razor pulse
of a nerve shooting
hip to heel to stop me
crossing the street—
A-live, a-live, shit, shit.

Here is the steam caress
on the face, the iron kiss
searing a hand smooth
as stone and erasing
freckles, fingerprints,
any sense of touch.

But here—however
unwilling—is the heart's
clenched fist pumping
its chambers free
of blood before
it can fill again.

THE WOLF AND THE KID

Uncle Dale slips the blade from the black ivory handle
and holds it by the tip. *That girl would have got along*
just fine with one of these right here. He flips it back
beside his ear then fires it dead center into the Y
in my mother's prized Queen Anne cherry.
I stare at the spot waiting for it to ooze like
a wound. He smells like gasoline and beer,
calls me *Sir* and expects the same even when
we're playing water pistol tag. *How about*
another soaking, Sir? Yes, sir! I would shriek.

He hands me the knife, says, *You can't count on*
your folks or me. My goose was cooked in the war.
I do not ask where he disappears to
for months at a time. I do not ask why
he sleeps in the truck or cries in his sleep.
I do not ask what he was doing with a goose
during the war. I take the knife and throw
without looking. It lands on the ground,
pins the stem of a daisy to the grass.
Uncle Dale sighs, *That shit'd be fine*
for flower picking but this here's the woods
and you are the hunted. You copy? I nod.
He holds the tip out again. Eyes half-shut,
I cock the knife back and throw again.
It pierces a smaller branch. He raps
my belly hard with his knuckle,
You stay here until you nail it.

An hour later, my arm burns and shakes.
In the little light left, I can hardly see the nicks
in the bark. They look like tiny birds ready
to take flight with the whole tree. I've hit
the mark several times, but it's always
one more. *Sir!* I say. *It's supper time.*
His gaze is slow to find me, the smile
even slower. He crushes a can between
his hands and promises to catch up
though he never follows me inside.
One by one, the nicks in the cherry tree
thicken over and darken like the scarred
hide of some great beast, lying in wait.

ST. ANTHONY'S BREAD

The whole bus tips right with his step
then left when he boards. My forehead
knocks the window where I've pressed my face
to watch boys skateboard up onto the brick
steps of Pioneer Square. In faded fatigues
the man lumbers down the aisle
with a yellow blanket tucked under his arm
like a baby he's ransacked from a stroller.
Anywhere but here, I repeat, until he's sitting
beside me, left leg pressing against mine
and hot. He unwraps a monstrous sandwich.
Lettuce flies onto the floor, the seat, the book
in my lap. The bread heel looms at my mouth
until I realize as it shakes that he's offering me
a bite of the thing. That's when I turn
and meet his gaze, and truly, except for
his nose and eyes the man is covered
in slick, black hair speckled with crumbs
and woven with lettuce right down
to the knuckles. His eclipsed eyes
give me vertigo. Between us, the smell
of yeast rises thick as pollen. Maybe
it's the sleepless nights, the empty house,
my vision swimming under his gaze,
the sun's warm spell through the window
working my neck and shoulders—
how else to explain why I believe him
when he swears one bite would right
the world. I do not flinch when
he tears off a chunk and extends
his open hand under my nose
as if I were a bird hovering
at the open window. I take
the bread in my mouth and hold it
like a promise, an offering, a secret
I will keep without knowing the terms.

SHOOTING RANGE

The first and only shot makes my palm
itch as if someone slapped my hand.
None of us can find where
the bullet goes. My brother slips
the gun from me and hands it
to my sister. The oily metallic air
blends with a carnival fried bread smell.

My sister takes aim and tags a shoulder.
The target flies up and settles back like
a tablecloth shaken of crumbs.
After catching someone in a black ski mask
race out our front door into a line of trees,
my brother joins the gun club. The eldest,
I don't tell him he's more likely to injure
one of us than stop an intruder.

The youngest, he'd only cite another fact
so wildly outrageous but true, it would stop
me cold. Like how Russian astronauts
take guns into space to shoot bears
in case they land off course. The middle child,
my sister would swear she'd heard that too.
I pass on my turn. My sister pulls the gun
to eye level. Skin flushed, she is
dark-eyed and beautiful and smirking
now that she's found something else
she does better than her sister.

Watch this, my brother says, the boy
who has been telling me for years I am not
his mother. In a few months, we'll scatter
like buckshot from the home we grew up in—
to college, an apartment, a marriage. Already,
we're promising to call, write, send pictures.
I watch their trained gazes, mouths open,
and hold my breath. My brother's bullet
strikes the red center. My sister whoops
and hollers as an alarm sounds.
The target speeds away from us.

SETTING THE FIRE

They couldn't even blame
what they'd done on a dare
or claim the boy on the corner—
rumored to have blinded
his own dog in one eye—
had forced their hands.
They had never seen
green flames before.
They watched the edges
of a pizza delivery ad blacken
then turn to ash and then
the blonde tresses of a girl
who'd gone missing long
before they were born.
They searched for the glossy pages
of magazines to conjure those witchy
shades, not seeing the red embers
settle into the dry brush
around them. When the hem
of the fire moved into dense brush,
they might have tamped it down
with their feet but the flames
rose, and the kids stood rooted
to the earth under a flickering spell—
the summer too full of itself
to let anything terrible happen.
A wall of heat climbed, birds
scattered overhead, wood
snapped and whined. Not
until the flames licked
the bright blue shell
of a tent did they look
away, not until smoke
snaked up the wall
of a cabin did they run.

THINGS I'VE TAKEN A MATCH TO

The ballerina in her jewelry box with a heart painted on the top. Picture frames and peach pits. Peppercorns and cracker jacks. The edges of a tractor tire. The rope holding the tire up in a tree in a neighbor kid's yard, the one who called my father a spic. A Barbie doll's leg. A snake husk. A teddy bear's green eye. A stink bug. Tinsel. A Christmas tree on New Year's Eve. A letter telling a man I was leaving him. A bale of straw. Hair spray. The Blue Frog Bar and Grill in River Town, Chicago, where I sang karaoke two weeks after my mother died. My body. Paper stuffed in a bottle of sugar cane schnapps. A destination. The barn windows the bottle burst through. The mown fields where the flames crawled. The house the flames reached. A map. The tent I was meant to sleep in. A rumor. A lie. A letter telling a man I was coming home. The good girl pulling the night up to her chin for cover, again and again and again.

AKATHORASBHAGARVAKOMALA, A VERY SOFT FABRIC

Running the fabric over her palm
at the bazaar, she releases her breath
the way a mother blows
on a sleeping child's forehead
in late summer's heat.
Held up to the sun, it warms
the stark light. She catches
the scent of fish brine, turmeric,
pani puri, and overripe tomatoes
she can never carry home
without bruising. Already
she can imagine her new husband
sitting up in bed in the other room
to tell her the fabric would cost
them a fortune, that it would
never do for a dress,
that she would only tear it
or choke the threads
with dust, grime, smoke.

She bought carnations once—
blood red blooms wrapped
in white butcher paper
smudged with dirty handprints.
She'd trimmed the stems, changed
the water every day and they kept
their color for weeks.
Now, in a warped window,
she catches a mask
of kohl-rimmed eyes—
her own—and asks the seller
to repeat the word
which gives her enough time
to roll the swatch she's torn
into a seed between her fingers.
She whispers the word
under her breath
until it hums like a hymn
she's known her whole life.

STARVING THE PANIC

Whatever woke you—
the baby choking, a lover's elbow

to your chin, mice scratching
Morse code between the walls behind

the bed, the rumor you never admitted
to starting, the doctor's *I'm sorry* before

she leaves the room—let it take one
last snap like a towel wound

and whipped at your thigh
in a high school locker room. And then

let it settle like a sheet. Set your hands
to smoothing each billow and pocket. Pull

the corners taut, lie back in the dark
as if you're waiting for someone

to join you for a midnight picnic, someone
who still hasn't shown by 1am, 2am, 3am,

and you hardly care anymore because
no matter what morning carries

in its silver hands, the moon
is a purple-tongued pup,

wagging the black night, just
begging you to throw something.

HEAT

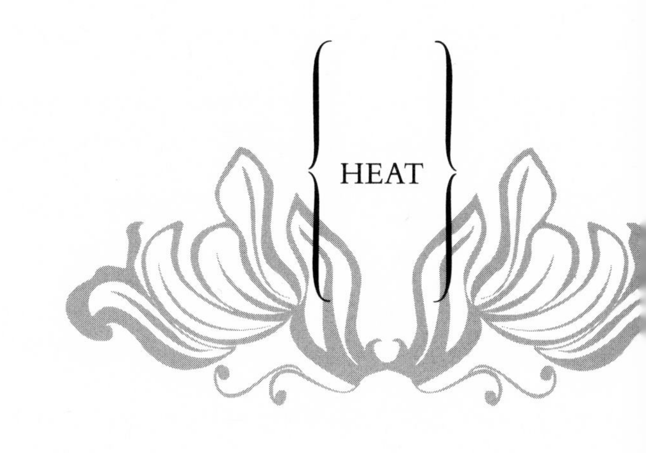

ST. MARY'S CATHOLIC SCHOOL FOR GIRLS

Regina Castellano says she heard it straight
from a penguin: sex means penetration,

so she can do anything and everything
but that and still slip through heaven's gates.

It's Friday, game day, party night.
In study hall, Regina putties on make-up

like her mother, rolls up her hem and holds it
in place with safety pins while Sister Lange snores.

She grips the glass top drawing table in the corner
and kisses the surface to show us how to work

our tongues. Her father's going to jail but Dad
says the real news is whether or not the boy

caught with her in the supply closet will play
football. Ricky James has yet to kiss me, says

he prefers nice girls, but admits to going
to after-game parties with the rest of the team.

He shrugs when I ask if he sees Gina there.
Monday morning in P.E., she laughs.

Nice girls are like Babe the Blue Ox. Total myth.
She unhooks her bra, pulls it out her sleeve

then sprints down the track. Even the lady
gym coach can't look away. In a training bra,

skin chafing against the uniform's
coarse restraint, I race to catch up.

THE DRIVER'S TEST

Clouds like cobwebs cling to morning
as I stand on the curb, stomach pitching
until Craig pulls up, not behind the wheel

of the bug I'd practiced in for weeks,
but a rusted-out pickup I would need a stool
to climb. The wind shifts direction, sets leaves

spinning at our feet where his litany
of apologies fall. I don't care what broke
in the bug or how late his father will be

for work because of me, I will hold this
against him for as long as we live. He shrugs
when I fail the test after denting the bumper

on a lamp post, drives home while I ride
in the truck bed letting the wind lift
the torn halves of my permit. Months

from now, some old bat will miss
a stop sign and fire him from his motorcycle
like something shot from a cannon over

telephone wires and into a sky so clear
and blue it burns to stare into. When
I finally pass the test, I'll drive that route

in my own truck, lights cut in the dark,
street empty as I fly through the intersection,
eyes shut, daring anyone to stop me.

THE FARRIER

Dad was a blunt-edged shovel of a man. A dry
spigot of a man. Mom running off with the farrier
made all the sense in the world. With his full beard
and chocolate gaze, he looked like a lean Grizzly Adams.

The only other time I saw Mom curl her hair
was for church and we hadn't been in years, not since
Dad started working second shift fixing tractors.
From the barn, I heard the soft whinnies of her laughter
as my mother stroked the horses' manes and the farrier

cradled one, then another hoof, his voice milky, *Easy.*
Easy now. Afternoons, I waited for him on the bumper
of his squat black truck with the silver horse head
on the hood searching intently for some distant finish line.

He greeted me with *Howdy Do, Little Lady.* I shared
the news that played all day and night from the barn,
like how it snowed in the Sahara Desert for thirty minutes
and gas prices were expected to hit $1.00 a gallon by summer.

He searched my eyes the way only the horses did as he shook
his head and whistled disbelief. Just once, I wanted him
to sit down for supper, chew the fat, then ride the horses so
hard beside us, their shoes would wear out and he'd have to stay.

ON THE ANNIVERSARY OF HER HUSBAND'S DEATH, GREAT AUNT IRENE CALLS

Did you notice the birch buds busting
through their downy shells? That frost due

this weekend will snap them at the neck, I swear.
He never noticed that sort of thing, shrugged

if I'd point it out. And the garden he never
wanted smack dab in the front yard

beside the driveway? Hell, no one minds
a bit though maybe one day the kids

will leave me a few strawberries.
I don't grieve the man except on walks

just before it rains, or when, in a rush,
I have to sit down to catch my breath. He

couldn't hurry from a forest fire. Drove me batty.
Like that time blood ran down our son's hands

and face and he saunters to the medicine cabinet
as if I'd asked him for mouthwash. It's not so bad

anymore. Even the talking to myself. *As long as you*
don't start answering, he used to say. *Too late*, I say.

Not a fan of these putty clouds but in this light,
I don't look so bad for my age. I suspect he'd still

want to jump my bones, though if anyone
did any jumping around here, it was me.

BLACKOUT

Outside of meal times, bingo, Chapel
Sundays, and Friday night films, Mr. Carnana
could never be left alone with Mrs. Dibella.

Five minutes was all it took for her
to wheel him into a closet even the nurses
had no idea existed. Once, a candy-striper

found them in another building for residents
with good mobility, memories intact.
Mrs. Dibella kneeled on a blanket

while he sat back, wide-eyed, mouth slung
open and gasping like a fish. Most days,
neither one can name the spouses

they've been married to their whole lives,
or their children, or their grandchildren
but Mrs. Dibella can recall an entire

summer detasseling corn in the Midwest,
the farm boys lined up in the grass
at dawn and ready for the mad harvest

before a storm, her new dress sewn
from her mother's Sunday church dress—
red pansies around blood-black hearts.

Mr. Carnana remembers how his father lost
a thumb in the meat slicer at the corner deli
on Kenmare on the Lower East Side.

His mother only flicked crumbs from her apron,
A little thinner, Daddo. After Pearl Harbor,
on nights without a moon, Mr. Carnana still

sees the cigarette bursts they followed block
to block to meet friends, still hears Artie Shaw's
"Stardust" tumbling from a club's open door.

Decades later, they no longer know daughters
or sons but they remember women pining
for men shipped overseas, too many returned

only to be buried. She says, *Tony, Roger, Pete.* He
says, *Greta, Betty, Delilah.* They kiss with their lips,
teeth, and tongue, all flesh and blood and bone.

HANSEL ALONE

A lifetime ago, arm in arm, they used to drift between the spruce and pine collecting mushrooms until that day they found the owl in the leaves, tufts wet, brooding face an omen. They buried it with all their child's grief and somewhere missed a turn. For three days, they hunted asparagus, wild strawberries, roses, and stripped bark from young willow shoots to eat them raw. They wove stories like webs from branches, gave life to creatures with rotted bark and moss, and slept in a bed of needles under a canopy of leaves. On the third day, he brushed lichen from her shoulder and kissed her on the mouth. She startled then kissed him back and as if a spell had broken, they found the familiar path. Now, he reaches the same spot winded, an old man. He finds the wide rock and tilts his face up to meet the rain. Here, he greets the same stunned silence they had as children, staring through the trees into the ruins of their lives, hanging back in the gathering dark, suspended in their wild.

THE REEL

Heads back, mouths wide, the men clutch
the woman between them, one gripping

her legs, the other her waist. In the next
frames, their bodies tip back and forth like

a mute bell. Their mouths open and shut, open
and shut. Mother called this sacred, for marriage

alone, but as I unrolled the film beneath a lamp,
I had to wonder which was the husband? What

simple math had they undone, these parents
who never touched, who hid the reel in a box

in the back of the closet? Again and again,
I returned to those bodies, swinging beneath

the disco lights, the men with black chest hair
wearing gold-rimmed sunglasses, the woman

swimming between them, pink and hairless, arms
raised as if diving frame to frame. I'd practice

staring at the ceiling, back arched, lips
opening along the length of my arm so

quiet and slow, I'd grow dizzy forgetting
to breathe. If no one ever kissed me

like that, I didn't care. I couldn't swim
either but I could hold my breath forever.

ANATOMY OF A GIRL

I.

Her father sits her down at the picnic table
the morning after her mother caught her
loping up the gravel drive, and lined
with evergreens swishing
that October night around
the heartsick thumping in her chest
after a date with a senior, and she only
a freshman. On the front porch, arms
crossed, feet tapping, her mother works
her gum. Her father puts a foot up
on the seat opposite her and sighs.
Look, he says, *men want one thing.*
You give it to them and you're a whore, okay?
She says nothing about the night before
or the boy or whether or not that makes
her a whore. Beyond them, a breeze
picks up, tugs at the evergreens.
Most of them are rust-colored
and dying, split down the middle,
smothering everything in their shade.

II.

As a girl, she remembers winning
a long distance race against the whole
third grade class and waiting to tell
her mother. She swung her legs
at the kitchen table as her mother opened
her nursing book. The faceless figures floated
on the page in pink with black lines. One
had polka dot nipples and a long penis
between them like a walking cane.
The other had wide smiles for breasts
and whiskers in her hips so it looked like
a cat peered out from her uterus.

Her mother dragged a finger under each word
as she said them aloud: *ovaries, vagina, clitoris,*
testes, pubis, vas deferens, penis, scrotum.
Something inserted, released, then
boom: baby. Her voice shifted
between nice nurse and gym coach
until the girl wondered whether to lie down
or run laps. *It's sacred, private*, her mother said.
The girl thinks about a neighbor, his
one gold tooth blinking down at her.

III.

The girl finds the words watching
the dirty old landlord chase Chrissie
around a sofa on *Three's Company. Mom,*
she says, *I have to tell you something.* Her mother
turns off the vacuum, picks at a spot
in the carpet. The girl whispers
his name. *He made a pass at me,*
she says. Her mother wants
to know what she means. *He chases me,*
the girl tells her. She has no words
for what he does when he catches her.
Her whole body feels so hot and light it rises
out of her clothes like a balloon
so that she's drifted far away by the time
her mother turns the vacuum back on.

WOMAN CLAIMS HEARING LOSS GIVES THE GIFT OF SIGHT

For weeks after the explosion, a velvet curtain
falls across her left ear with a hummingbird's
thrum behind it. She hears a ticking

with every spoken word like something hot
left to cool. She studies the concert of mouths,
cheeks, and chins, how the light in someone's eyes

falls like water with a sigh or blooms with a laugh,
and the movement of hands—waving, clenched,
flattened in a lap, or tapping time against

a thigh. The whole body conducts a story
and she sees for the first time that the neighbor
would rather she stay in the drive than walk

around the hedge to exchange news. When
she's watering plants outside, the mail carrier
would still prefer to put the mail through the door slot

than place it in her hands. One afternoon,
she watches her lover come home, eyes trained
not on her sitting in a lawn chair but on the grass,

his steps careful as if a sudden dip might
sink him. He glances over her and smiles.
A wave breaks in her ear and she can see

his face open like a page in a book,
the faint words fluttering and weightless.

THE QUARRY

Great slabs of concrete along the shore
made rigid diving boards but after

Midwest storms, the quarry offered
the only escape from the wool net

of humidity. Kids made out
in rusted cars, sold dope on washers

and stoves, surrounded by feral kittens
and abandoned dogs. The chemical plant

dumped mill tailings from waste, whatever
residents hadn't already taken free as landfill.

Gases blown into town turned the windows
blue and corn borers ate into the curtains.

The boys dove as the girls tanned their skin
to a burnt sugar, lightened their honey hair

with peroxide, unraveled long limbs
from their child bodies like strands

from a braid. Faces flushed, the girls smoked
joints then hunted for clusters of tadpoles

in the black sand, giggling when the boys
tried to sneak up on them from under water.

After dark, hand in hand, bodies ablaze,
they rose like gods across the rocks.

HEAT

As the heat climbs, the road falls off the distance into a shimmering blue pool we race to but never reach. Mesquite, wild oats, and orange poppy clouds chuff along beside us. Dizzy with the static view, I pull over to let you drive and stare at your profile until your face blurs and you turn into the drifter we passed two miles back—a man with the look of a worn saddle set on a half-wild horse. We meant to push on to be home by dark, but convince ourselves to escape the devil winds by driving to a town whose only draw is underground caves where pink salamanders navigate without eyes and translucent millipedes move unseen in the rocks. We skirt stalagmites down the steps, swirl our hands in the water. Something like a moth flutters at my ankle. The guide turns out the lamp to reveal pitch black. I edge us into a hollow. You don't tell me to stop, but slip your hands up my shirt, a bedrock grip to keep me still. Arms around your neck, I hold us steady. Miles above, the drifter flicks a cigarette to the wind.

WARDING OFF A PROPOSAL

Charming woman, empty gourd.
Spanish Proverb

Serve bitter almond cookies made with twice
the salt, half the required butter. When he asks

for water, cup one ear and make him repeat
the request until you clap your hands

over your mouth in shock. From the kitchen,
hum a wedding tune, fill the jug if you like, clink

the glasses together like a bell tolling the hour.
Wander out back into the herb garden

your father built for your mother, surrounded
by wild plum and fig trees. Lie down in the grass

where you hid eggs at Easter only to find
a few while planting seeds in summer.

Here, you built a fortress of leaves, painted
ladybugs on rocks, named caterpillars Manuel,

Manuel I, Manuel II after a favorite uncle, and stood
rooted as a bulb when your father told you he had

just a few months to live but would leave you
everything, so you need only marry for love.

Pick an unripe gourd and bring it back
to the living room where you have made

him wait. If he asks about the water, offer
the gourd. If he asks again, invite him to supper.

ONCE UPON A TIME

I pitched a tent in a yard in Seville
beside a one-eyed goat. A lemon curtain
fluttered in the window, solid and brilliant

enough to hold the whole crumbling
house up. The sky cast a pearly glow
on the grass. When I stepped inside,

my lover sat at an antique lathe working
blocks of wood into chess pieces. A horse,
a knight, one pawn after another. *Where*

are the children? I asked. *I unmade them*
for you, he said, black curls writhing along
his cheek as his foot tapped the pedal, thumbs

turning the wood in swift circles. *But not to worry,*
he winked, *we can always make them back.* Clouds
ran between us. His hair grayed into smoke.

His knuckles swelled and knotted, the body
he once wore flew into the distance like
a tattered shirt as the tent collapsed. Feet

on the grass, my body shed the girl, grew
thick and heavy as if I'd come ashore after
a long swim. From inside, he pulled back

the curtain and waved me in for cold soup
and day old bread. I hadn't felt hunger
in years and didn't want to come inside

but somewhere on the wind I heard
the children's voices gathering like birds.
Cicadas swam up from Catalpa roots

and hummed themselves to life. The tent
became a sheet in my hand. As soon as
I folded it, the grandchildren raced up,

our children smiling behind them.
My lover shuffled out to greet them.
In my pocket, I still held the Queen.

BREATH

AFTER THE FIRE

Rain pelts the bottom of the bucket
where my sons collected worms
to prod and poke and scare
the girl on the corner
who never shares
her gum. The worms
recoil from the downpour,
flattening beneath
explosive plunks. One rolls
up over another as if to soften the blow.

I swirl the water slowly
and walk next door where
ruderal weeds sprout
through the black earth,
scorched after a boy tucked
a blanket in the gas fireplace grate
to make a fort. The framing
survived except for
one wall, as if the house
always meant to open onto
the wetland where the sun sets.

In a back bedroom with an infant
whose slightest cough woke me,
I slept through the burning
timber, the second floor
folding onto the first like a lid,
the windows exploding,
the wail of sirens,
and the coyote who kept up
the call that roused me finally
to the trees reflecting light.

Black glass shards still litter
the ground. I empty the bucket
where a few grass bouquets
have gathered. The worms
writhe toward escape, their arterial
stretches and bends readying
to till the earth, return
root to its shrub, blade
to grass, bulb to bud. If
only they could knit back the boy.

IN COLLEGE, I JOB SHADOW MY MOTHER, A HOSPICE NURSE

and meet an entire family in their kitchen drinking honey
spiced vodka while sauerkraut soup cooks on the stove.

On the counter, slices of poppyseed cake attract fruit flies.
My mother has never drunk the hard stuff, but here

she tosses one back and hums her approval
before wandering into the dining room

where Bogdan sleeps in an enormous bed propped
against a hutch. From the kitchen, they pose questions

in English, respond in Ukrainian. A woman hollers,
Who hasn't embezzled Chicago? A deep voice barks,

Tell me this, what homosexuals need their own parade for?
My mother checks the IV, inspects pill bottles,

instructs me to write down the pulse and blood pressure
as their laughter erupts. The house reeks of sweat

and rubbing alcohol. *You are sympathetic to homosexuals,*
no? A throaty tenor settles at my shoulder like

an enormous bird. My mother groans, rolls her eyes
as I flinch and face a towering figure. A white spot

on his top lip forms a line like a tightrope
to the bottom when he speaks. *You're college girl*

but mother's daughter. And she is angel. We forgive you.
He fires in his native tongue to a woman who leaps

from her chair to pour vodka into two blue cups.
She hands one to me. The man takes the other

and says, *Bogdan, means gift from God.* He holds
his cup out for a toast. I do the same. *But now,*

he says, *we send him back.* His howl flies out
in a lengthy wheeze, silent at the end

until he catches his breath back to wheeze again.
My mother slaps her chest laughing. The vodka

burns all the way down. Bogdan never stirs.

THE USES OF GRIEF

No one will ask you to house sit or walk the dog
while they frolic on the shores of Hawaii—

most likely, they will never even tell you
they are going. Friends will not resist

when you pull away from a hug but nearly squeeze
you dry if you initiate. And whether it's for sex

or a carnival ride, no one will try to set
the mood or coax you into going.

Neighbors will not expect you
at the annual BBQ, but if you come,

they'll be delighted you didn't trouble yourself
to cook something. They'll refill your drinks

unasked even as they count how many
you suck down. No one will ask to borrow

a cup of sugar or a rake, much less expect you
at book club, birthday parties, baby showers.

People you hardly know will pray for you,
and though you have no idea what you believe,

when you growl about asking God to do something
useful, like pulling weeds or laundry, you will

wake to find someone has pulled the weeds.
Maybe it's only the fear that someone

like your mother will show up to do
your laundry, but you finally stuff a pile

of clothes into the washer. Then, one day,
a sorrow newer than yours sends you

to someone else's doorstep with your best lasagna
and a bottle of whiskey, and you walk right in

because you know she will not protest, not
when you rummage the cabinets or pour drinks,

not when you reheat the food, or set it down
in front of her on a cracked orange plate.

THE EDGE OF SPRING

A few inches beneath the frosted surface,
the dirt warms and thickens, more
like modeling clay or wet cement
than anything a root
could plumb. The blue blood
evening drags the afternoon
behind it like an unwilling bride.
This is the time of year to plant garlic,
to line the sills with plastic trays
of seedlings. This is the time
of year children refuse
their jackets because the sun's out
only to wind up sick in bed
the next weekend when the weather
really turns. This is the time of year
I see your casket lowering
into that muck. I'd snuck in
a fistful of seeds for each shovelful
of dirt—grass, flowers, creeping vines, peas
and carrots, something as slow and weighted
as this grief. Something to break up
the grid of monuments and grass.
Something as sudden and enduring
as my laughter at the thought of carrots
sprouting at the foot of your headstone.

THE DIFFICULT HABIT OF STAYING ALIVE

Mud spattered, muscles taut as leather
over its bones, the horse races through a field
of waist-high wheat. An ancient woman rides

the horse bareback, a braid of gray birds
fluttering at her back. I've been drinking,
though why it matters, I don't know.

Her gaze holds mine, looms closer and closer.
The horse makes no effort to slow, looks like
it will plow right through me until it stops,

frozen against the steel sky, a sudden still life.
Without moving her mouth, the woman
speaks, *It's your time.* I look her

in the eye but cannot fix on her face, only
the striped grainy quality of it, solid as driftwood.
I defend my life's worth, but every reason falls

like a poorly made paper plane onto
the hard-packed earth. I have nothing
she wants that I am willing to barter.

At last, I say, *I'm not ready.* A wave breaks
against my sternum, threatens to flatten me
like an offering at her feet. When I wake,

I'm stunned, muscles electric with fear, heart
pounding like those hooves in the distance.
It was only a dream, I recite, *only a dream,*

my body as sure and real as my son's
smile. But all day, the air smells
acrid as burning leaves, the winds

shift direction, the sky bears the same
bruised shadows wherever I go.

BREATH

Saturday night and the hours spiral
like dominoes into a morning covered
in the same patchy fog as my new
mother's brain. Something's wrong
with the baby. Something in the tight bee swarm
cough, the fists each time I lay him down. Maybe
it's nothing, like these unsettling marine clouds
the morning will burn through. *Probably*
it's nothing, I hear in the voice
of my grandmother, my mother,
the wind pushing leaves
in the same small circles
in the street. Outside, a deer slinks up
along the side of the house to chew
the tulip bulbs between bars of soap
a neighbor laid out to ward her off.
She used to come with a fawn
but now, alone, there is a singed divot
where one eye used to be. The other
pins me in the room.
The baby's lip turns a deep wormy purple.
I whisper a prayer then hold my breath
as if my breath were all I would give.

MOTION STUDY

I.
The bird smacks
into the sliding glass doors,
thunks to the deck, heart flitting
like another bird lurking
beneath its breast. The eye
facing up takes everything
in and holds it there. A Stellar's Jay
trots up to investigate before flying off.
With its heart ready to burst,
I have no right to touch it,
but on hands and knees I crawl
holding my breath, and stretch
an arm out, then one finger
toward the curved flame
of its tiny red claw.
The sharp point
tugs a callous
and I'm caught in the act—
the wrong, the worship.

II.
In some fantasies,
I am faster than the car
blazing into the cul-de-sac,
music trailing from each
open window like torn scarves.
My son listens, for once, to the bark
and boom of my drill sergeant
voice. The song ends. A prop plane
flies past so low markings emerge
along its belly—a code
unraveling the day.
Across the pavement:
a shadow like a manta ray
cruising the shoreline.
On the curb: hollow thump
thump as the bumper strikes
a dog. In the grass:
my boy gets to his feet.

THIS BOY, HERE

We watch the rat list side to side
in its cage. Its eyes shut then snap
open again like a spring. Any

moment now, the thing will drop
for good. When it does, my son asks,
Why? Rats only live three years, I say.

He insists, *Why? I don't know.*
At four, he figures that makes him
older than any living rat on the planet.

Satisfied, he gathers stuffed animals
around him to play while I'm left
to dispose of the body. Outside,

a full moon swells as if it will
eventually fill the street like
dough rising. I pull a rock up,

dig beneath the gravel and lay
the rat down in an old gym sock—
a snug tight tomb. Back inside,

I wash my hands and sit down beside
my son, who doesn't ask where I've been
and never mentions the rat. Months

before, he had asked if when you die,
you could come back. *Some people*
think so, I told him. We imagined

how we might return, he as a cloud,
a shark, a knight, a guinea pig named
Snowy, me as a bird, a tree, a queen,

a purple anemone. Now, he makes
me swear to come back as myself, as
just his mother. *And I will come back*

as just me, he says, the one hand
patting his chest, the other pulling
my chin to face him, *This boy, here.*

THROUGH THE FIRE

From the buzz saw voice
crackling on the answering machine
only a few words make sense:
It's an emergency. My arms let go of books,
the mail. I race down the block.

On the way, I meet my husband
at the scene of an accident,
my son floating at the edge
of a lake, an aunt fallen down
a stairwell, my mother, in the throes
of a heart attack, and still wearing the pink slippers
I sent for her birthday. I watch myself
collapse at each scene, each future

opening like a break in the clouds: skin
thinning against bone, the whiskey
burning my cheeks, the house
consumed by cobwebs,
a name written in the dust on the table
where I used to paint,
the afternoons stacked like
blank canvases in a corner.
By the time I bang on her door, I am

an old woman struggling up the porch,
out of breath, hands trembling, legs unsteady.
Then her eyes meet mine and I understand.
The crisis: no one I know.
The wreck: a friend of a friend.
The tragedy: relief.
I put an arm around her shoulder, agree
to watch her children, tongue clicking, voice
humming consolation even as I pull

my husband from the wreckage, drag
my son onto shore, sit my aunt
back down on the bar stool
and order a round for the house.

THE LAMP

The lamp had been a wedding gift to my mother
from her mother, who failed to talk her daughter
out of the marriage. We changed the shade
with every move—a pea green cotton
in an apartment in the 70s, an ivory lace
with scalloped trim in the summer cottage
that had no working plumbing, or the red plaid
after we lost the house and agreed to work
a horse farm in exchange for rent. My father

fell for the boarders, women in black who wore
boots to their knees, called him Ricky Ricardo,
and rode the horses until they foamed
at the mouth, their manes dripping sweat.
Once, when he'd disappeared after supper,
my mother stormed out to the barn,
and returned with the lamp he'd dragged
out there one night to repair a tractor.

If he wants to live there, she said, *he can
sleep there*. By day she restored the house,
painting room after room, yanking the lamp
behind her by the cord until the wires split
from the head. At night, she held the bare bulb
beside her face and told us bedtime stories
about bigfoot searching the woods
for his long lost love, and the half wolf,
half woman who haunted the creek after
dark to keep children from drowning.

Years later, I find the lamp in the trash
only a few weeks after my mother's death.
From the brass base to the white glass vase
with roses blooming in relief across its surface,
it is light in my hand and missing a shade.
My father shakes his head, *That thing
is a hundred years old. It was hers,* I return.
I take the lamp home, pore over the pages
of books by it, rubbing the surface as I turn it
off to sleep. The glow shrinks down to a point
then winks out like a genie tucked safe inside.

THE LAST TO GO

Humans are ... capable of detecting certain substances in dilutions of less than one part in several billion parts of air.
Social Issues Research Center

The one part should be a lover's shirt
under the bed, fueling lewd dreams, not
towels from the dog's bath. But if the part

of the brain ruling the slippery terrain
of emotion and memory also houses
our sense of smell, we can no more choose

than avoid what binds us to a moment.
A childhood leaping hay bales and cornering
chipmunks in a barn can wash off like finger

paint when I pass a garage and smell
the metal odor of my father's hands, nails
black, skin cut as he unbuckled his belt.

Never mind that his hands in summer
also smell of overripe plums. I cannot bite
down on a scent to test its purity or stop

it the way a photo does a moment. I cannot
grip a smell or hold it down until it screams
Uncle! and tells me what it wants, where

it's been, and what it will do when I let it go.
We may be rare mammals to contemplate
death but if we ever saw it coming, not

anymore; now, we recoil from its brine and oil
as if we could thwart death with proper hygiene,
good breeding, salt thrown over one shoulder.

I want to greet it with a firm handshake
and an offer of tea. As memories slipped like
balloons from a child's wrist, I'd want to remember

a life of scents: the lemon vodka a friend poured
the last time we spoke, the rose powder that never
hid my mother's cigarettes, my lover's soapy salt

lovemaking, my son's musk sweat when he woke
blue-lipped with croup, that mint-cold winter,
summers of chlorine and lilac, basil and blood.

THE DAY AN OFFICER SHOWS UP WHO LOOKS EXACTLY LIKE THE ACTOR GARY OLDMAN

Not when he played a one-eyed pimp
with a gold grille, long opaque nails,

and a scythe scarred around his cheekbone.
Not the gay playwright done in by his lover.

Not the crooked cop in a white suit who blasts
through an apartment door and everyone

moving behind it as he hums Moonlight Sonata.
No, I'm talking about the one where he plays

Beethoven opposite Isabella Rossellini,
and the bombs fall as his hearing slips

like an unmoored boat, and anguish distorts
his features as he spends the rest of his life

composing under water. He's the one
knocking on the front door as the toast

sticks in my throat and I list all the things
I fear he's about to tell me, weighing

the chances he's only come to ask
for a donation. When I return again

and again to that morning when grief
split my world into a triptych—

before and after and the heart stop between—
it's a different face I prepare to greet him:

the petite blonde with the high
ass he's hired out to a bachelor party,

the rich patron he owes everything, the man
who watches him sleep at night, the child

who witnessed his crime, or the woman
he's loved in secret his whole life.

UNWANTED PEPPER

I pull her sweatshirt on for the third day in a row
and yank the radishes out to expose their flaming heads.

Left in the ground too long, the insides turn fibrous
and mottled, even wooden. I could never

remember when to harvest despite all the work
of readying the soil, planting, watering. *It's like*

trying to read men, I'd said to my mother once,
the right shape and color, then you take a bite

and it's all unwanted pepper. She had rolled
her eyes, folded her hands around mine to show me

how to gather the dirt into piles into rows into which
she made a divot with her thumb for the seed

as if I were still a child. Some of the radishes make
a popping sound when my teeth break the surface.

Some I can't cut through with a knife. Others
never really grew, their little hearts as starved

as my mother's. Crows caw high in the pine trees,
carrying her voice, suppressing her laughter

when she'd finally inspected my finished work,
Even a weed couldn't sink a root in that mess.

THE RED EYE

Yellow globes strung like
Christmas lights along the highway

blink between wind-waved trees.
Half the world covered

in dark at an hour even regret
lies fast asleep and twitching like a dog.

How easy to imagine leaving
for good on a morning

as uncluttered and crisp
as this one. How clear the logic

of the dark: go now.
The roof will still hold.

Food will find its way
hand to mouth. The children

tucked in at home will grow old,
with or without a mother. And you,

with your hands gripping the wheel,
will still arrive with the morning.

DARK MATTER

Invisible to the eye, emits
no light. Galaxies cluster and turn
on hidden spindles. Scientists
count stars, gauge dust and gas
but the math never adds up—
the missing mass
like the missing limbs
of a primordial creature
whose shape we can only guess,
the gravitational force of a space
after a loved one's gone,
and how hard it is to breathe
despite a breeze from a window.

Days spin out weeks then months
then years, expanding into the vast
universe of grief. You search
for clues in drawers, cupboards,
pants pockets, coat pockets,
boxes, bags. You flip
through files, drawers, photo albums.
There is her face in a frame and here
pressed in the pages of a book,
blue flowers with purple tips,
and there in her careful handwriting
a recipe for potato pear soup.
In the sky, starlight fires
through unseen energy.
By the time the light
reaches you, some of the stars
are still alive, some long dead—
a difference you can never tell.

A SAGE ADVISES HOW TO FIREWALK

First thing in the morning, set a fire down
like a carpet over the lawn, in the spot
you might put a garden before summer's out
if you could get your act together. When

the flames die down to embers, use a rake
to spread them in a long pit. Do not lay
string or measure. And if you must know,
the temperature of those coals will exceed

1200 degrees. But this will mean
little to you when, from ten feet away,
the heat singes your eyelids. You don't
have to be a swami in a loincloth to make it

from one end to the other without toasting
your heels. And while interesting, it does
not help to know that when two bodies
of different temperatures meet, the hotter

of the two will cool off, while the cooler
of the two will heat up until the temperatures
match. And despite the testimonials, I swear

you don't need faith to carry you
safely across. Did you not dive into water
you couldn't see into? Dare a first kiss?
Drive home after one too many and keep

the car between the lines? Or swerve
to avoid the drunk? You buried a friend.
You pulled the child back onto the curb.
You did not strike back. You finally left

that dizzy bitch. Despite the new scar
like a jagged stitch across your chest, you
pulled that shirt off in broad daylight with
no clue how he might react. You said no.

You said yes. You stayed. You quit.
I'm here to tell you: you've got this.

NOTES

"Halloween, Baptist Church, Canton, NC" *In 2009, in Canton, NC, a Baptist Church celebrated Halloween by burning bibles that were not the King James Version, as well as music and books the congregation considered a satanic influence.*

"Savyiore" *For Dave Boersema*

"The Wolf and the Kid" *For Donald Sander, who is the kid and the wolf, the knife and the tree.*

"Akathorasbagharvakomala, A Very Soft Fabric" *For Pat Phillips West*

"The Quarry" *refers to West Chicago, Illinois where, from 1932 to 1973, a plant called Kerr McGee stored sand-like waste materials known as mill tailings that were made available free to residents as landfill from the 1930s through the 1950s, and also used to landscape and fill low-lying areas of town. The material was radioactive and hazardous, but the cleanup didn't begin until 1994 because of legal battles.*

"Once Upon a Time" *For Eddie Stange*

"Blackout" *For Cayla Davis*

"The Uses of Grief" *For Sue Lorrance*

"The Edge of Spring" *For Craig Kafar*

"The Difficult Habit of Staying Alive" *The title of this poem comes from a line in the poem "Damages" by Ruby Rahman.*

"Motion Study" *For Sandy*

"Dark Matter" *For Samantha Kitchen*

"A Sage Advises How to Firewalk" *For Diana Pagán and Edward Pagán.*

ACKNOWLEDGMENTS

Specials thanks to the following publications that published individual poems, sometimes in an altered format:

After Hours: A Chicago Journal of Art and Literature: "The Wolf and the Kid," formerly "Little Red Riding Hood"

Calyx: "Anatomy of a Girl"

Embers / Flames, An Anthology. Dyer, IN: Outrider Press, 2015: "How It All Started"

Field Magazine: "The Day An Officer Shows Up Who Looks Exactly Like the Actor Gary Oldman"

From the Depths: "Dark Matter" and "Things I've Taken a Match To"

Jet Fuel Review: "A Sage Advises How to Firewalk" and "The Uses of Grief"

Lake Effect: "Razbliuto"

New Verse News: "Wife Still a Suspect in Blaze that Claims Husband," formerly "Wife Still Sought for Questioning in Blaze"

Poet Lore: "The Reel"

Prick of the Spindle: "This Boy, Here" which was selected for *Best of the Net.*

San Pedro River Review: "The Farrier"

Tar River Poetry: "Unwanted Pepper"

The Madison Review: "The Edge of Spring"

VoiceCatcher: "Savyiore," formerly "Mail Call" which was nominated for a Pushcart Prize.

My immense thanks to The Broads—Phyllis Brown, Heidi Beierle, Mary Kibbe, and Pat Phillips West—whose input, friendship, and inspiration shaped this manuscript and sustained me. My gratitude to the collective members and editors at Airlie Press for their patience, wisdom, and editorial insights. Thank you to Beth Ford for her incredible artistic vision and design of the book's layout and cover. Catherine Bull, Jeremy Trabue, and Jan VanStavern also read through many early drafts of these poems for which I am very grateful. Thanks to the members of Awful Coffee, Michael Alleman, Sean Cotter, Kenneth Elliott, Fabian Iriarte, Tracey Mahon, and Simone Roberts for their early encouragement and support. My gratitude also goes to Amy Marie Young, whose short life inspired me to focus on what matters most every day. Thanks to Lucy Morrison for her moral support and enduring friendship. Thanks to Diana and Edward Pagán for their compassionate counsel and open hearts. My thanks go to my father for answering my never-ending questions, few of them easy. Thanks especially to my mother, whose spirit and laughter filter through every page of this manuscript. And finally, my immeasurable appreciation and boundless love to Jamie, Tristen, and Blaine, who have loved me unconditionally and tolerated my absences and distractions over these many years as I wrote and revised to make this book real.

ABOUT THE PUBLISHER

Airlie Press is run by writers. A nonprofit publishing collective, the press is dedicated to producing beautiful and compelling books of poetry. Its mission is to offer a shared-work publishing alternative for writers working in the Pacific Northwest. Airlie Press is supported by book sales and donations. All funds return to the press for the creation of new books of poetry.

COLOPHON

Titles and text are set in Bembo, a 20th-century revival of an old style humanist typeface cut by Francesco Griffo around 1495. It is named for the poet Pietro Bembo, an edition of whose writing was its first use.

Printed in the U.S.A. by Thomson-Shore on 30% post-consumer recycled paper, processed chlorine-free.